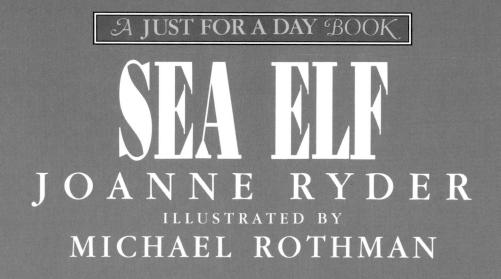

A JUST FOR A DAY BOOK

SEA ELF

JOANNE RYDER

ILLUSTRATED BY

MICHAEL ROTHMAN

MORROW JUNIOR BOOKS / NEW YORK

Special thanks to Dr. Marianne Riedman,
Director of the Sea Otter Field Research
Program, Monterey Bay Aquarium, for her
expert reading of this manuscript.

AUTHOR'S NOTE

Sea otters (*Enhydra lutris*) are marine mammals that live in the northern Pacific Ocean near the rocky coasts of Russia, Alaska, and California. These curious, playful creatures spend most or all of their lives in the waters near shore, where they can swim, hunt, sleep, mate, and bear their young.

In the past, hundreds of thousands of otters were slaughtered for their luxurious fur. Now protected, they are thriving in the northern parts of their range. A much smaller population, still threatened, lives off central California, and this book describes a day of a young otter in a cove near Point Lobos.

Sea otters—unlike whales and seals—have no thick layer of fat, or blubber, to protect them from the cold seas. They frequently groom their fur, trapping air bubbles inside for insulation. Clean fur keeps their skin dry and warm. An oil spill can be life-threatening to otters. They cannot clean the toxic oil from their fur and as a result die from the cold.

Undersea forests of giant kelp provide sea otters with shelter and food. They wrap the long blades of kelp around their bodies to anchor themselves in the ever-moving seas. By eating the sea urchins that destroy the kelp's rootlike holdfasts, sea otters protect the life-supporting forests where many creatures dwell and seek food.

Though otters hunt independently, a group, or raft, of otters often rest together in the kelp. A raft of female otters may include mothers with pups. Each mother otter carefully watches over her pup for six months or more. Then the young or juvenile otter is able to take care of itself.

Sea otters share the protected bays and coves near shore with many creatures—including sea gulls, cormorants, harbor seals, sea lions, and, on rarer occasions, visiting gray whales on their seasonal migrations along the California coast.

Acrylic paint was used for the full-color artwork. The text type is 14-point ITC Garamond Book.

Printed in the United States of America.
1 2 3 4 5 6 7 8 9 10

Library of Congress Cataloging-in-Publication Data
Ryder, Joanne. Sea elf / Joanne Ryder ; illustrated by Michael Rothman.   p. cm.—(A Just for a day book)
Summary: As a young sea otter, the reader enjoys a day of hunting, grooming, and playing in a California cove.
ISBN 0-688-10060-0.—ISBN 0-688-10061-9 (lib. bdg.) 1. Sea otter—Juvenile fiction. [1. Sea otter—Fiction. 2. Otters—Fiction.]
I. Rothman, Michael, ill. II. Title. III. Series. PZ10.3.R954Se 1993 [E]—dc20 92-27608 CIP AC

One chilly morning
gray fog
fills your room.
You snuggle
in covers
for warmth
from the coolness
that changes you
and your world.
Then....

You are soft,
warm and furry,
floating
in grayness.
Wrapped
in a blanket
of seaweed,
you bob
up and down
on a fog-covered sea.

With a flash
of your flippers,
you slide through
the waves rolling
closer and closer
to shore.
You glide
in your small, rocky cove,
looking up
at the sky turning blue
as the fog melts away.
Morning, Otter!

You take
a long breath
and dive deep
through a forest
hidden in the sea.
Golden towers
of kelp sway
around you.
Bubbles of air
rise from
your fur
like a trail
to the brightness
above.

You swim
near the shadowy
floor of the sea,
your paws
patting boulders,
touching feathery weeds.
You are hunting
for sea creatures
hidden in shells
who cling to the
weed-covered rocks.
You pluck them
and tuck each
one of your treasures
inside furry pouches
under your arms.
Then....

Breathless,
you soar
up and up
past darting crabs
and schools
of shining fish
to the place
where the sea
meets the sky.

Tap…tap…tap…
tap…tap…tap….
In the quiet cove
everyone knows
an otter is eating,
tapping pointy snails,
tapping spiky urchins.
You crack them
on a stone
on your soft belly,
breaking open
the breakfast
you found far below.

All through
the bright morning,
you hunt and you carry
red abalone
you eat from
its pearly plate.
Softly you coo
tasting
the salty goodness
tucked inside.
Then....

After you eat
you roll and roll
in the water,
cleaning your fur
as otters do.
You are an otter
among others
cleaning themselves
in the sea.

Your thick brown fur
fits like a big loose coat.
Inside it you curl,
reaching this way
and that way,
licking your fur,
rubbing it clean,
fluffing it full of air
so you can float
warm and dry
on the cold sea.

With small
mittenlike paws,
you rub and rub—
your head,
your ears,
your long, long whiskers,
till you
are clean
and fluffy-faced.

Sleepy otter,
you wrap yourself
in blankets of kelp
and close your eyes.
You sleep
on your floating bed
with your flippers
folded high,
warm and dry.

All around you,
others are napping,
some holding pups
safe on their chests.
Like tiny ships
you float together,
a raft of otters
smoothly rocking
on the sparkling sea.

You drift gently…
till tiny paws
tickle your face
and pat your chin.
A frisky pup
is teasing
you to play.

Together
you roll,
a fast ball
of brown fur
and flippers
playing
who-can-catch-who
and *which-tail-is-which*.
You spin and spin
till his mother
lifts him away,
and you watch
him ride off,
afloat on her chest.

On this calm, cool day,
you are a sea otter,
swift and sleek,
hunting and grooming,
playing and resting
at the edge of the sea.
All around you
creatures with fins
and with flippers
glide through
the forest of kelp.
Some live here too,
and others come
from far away.

Near you
the sea
explodes.
You sit up
on the water,
curious to see
someone new,
someone large,
making ripples,
making waves
as she passes by.
Strangers,
you share
this hidden cove
without harm.

Evening fog
slides across the sea,
hiding the sky,
filling the cove,
wrapping you up
in its grayness.
Rub your eyes
with your paws
till....

You see
your own room
warm and bright
all around you.
In your own bed,
so steady, so firm,
you snuggle
and dream
of flickering fish
and shadowy forests
and bright treasures
hidden within.